COUNTRY

Formal Name: Kingdom of Nepal ("Nepal Adhirajya" in Nepali).

Short Form: Nepal.

Term for Citizen(s): Nepalese.

Capital: Kathmandu.

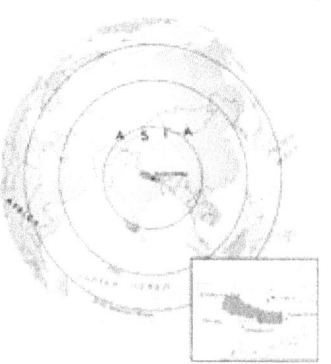

Click to Enlarge Image

Major Cities: According to the 2001 census, only Kathmandu had a population of more than 500,000. The only other cities with more than 100,000 inhabitants were Biratnagar, Birgunj, Lalitpur, and Pokhara.

Independence: In 1768 Prithvi Narayan Shah unified a number of states in the Kathmandu Valley under the Kingdom of Gorkha. Nepal recognizes National Unity Day (January 11) to commemorate this achievement.

Public Holidays: Numerous holidays and religious festivals are observed in particular regions and by particular religions. Holiday dates also may vary by year and locality as a result of the multiple calendars in use—including two solar and three lunar calendars—and different astrological calculations by religious authorities. In fact, holidays may not be observed if religious authorities deem the date to be inauspicious for a specific year.

The following holidays are observed nationwide: Sahid Diwash (Martyrs' Day; movable date in January); National Unity Day and birthday of Prithvi Narayan Shah (January 11); Maha Shiva Ratri (Great Shiva's Night, movable date in February or March); Rashtriya Prajatantra Diwash (National Democracy Day, movable date in February); Falgu Purnima, or Holi (movable date in February or March); Ram Nawami (Rama's Birthday, movable date in March or April); Nepali New Year (movable date in April); Buddha's Birthday (movable date in April or May); King Gyanendra's Birthday (July 7); Janai Purnima (Sacred Thread Ceremony, movable date in August); Children's Day (movable date in August); Dashain (Durga Puja Festival, movable set of five days over a 15-day period in September or October); Diwali/Tihar (Festival of Lights and Laxmi Puja, movable set of five days in October); and Sambhidhan Diwash (Constitution Day, movable date in November).

Flag: The national flag consists of two vertically stacked crimson red triangles with blue borders. The upper portion has an eight-pointed disc rising out of a white crescent moon, and the bottom portion has a white sun. The moon and sun symbolize the eternal eyes of god, the red color represents energy in action, and the blue border signifies Nepal's peaceful nature.

Click to Enlarge Image

1

HISTORICAL BACKGROUND

Early History: Available evidence of Nepal's distant past is scant, but the earliest inhabitants were likely of Tibeto-Burman ethnicity and lived in small settlements with little political centralization. Small kingdoms and tribal confederations controlled various areas of the Tarai Region in the south. Among these groups was the Sakya clan, whose most renowned member was Gautama Siddhartha, the Buddha, born in Lumbini in 563 B.C. Many historians believe the Kathmandu Valley's first rulers were the Gopals or Abhiras, followed by the Kiratas, who reigned until around A.D. 400, and then the Licchavis, who ruled from the late fifth century to approximately A.D. 750. Kings ("maharajas") of the Licchavi Dynasty ostensibly were both absolute political and moral authorities but had little influence on their subjects' lives. Their control over their territory and citizens relied on nobles who controlled private armies and large landholdings, and who in turn often influenced the royal court. In addition, village and caste councils often managed local administrative issues and had far greater ideological influence over subjects than Licchavi kings.

Medieval Nepal, 750–1750: After the Licchavi Dynasty, cultural and political changes occurred that would have enduring influences on Nepal. There was a shift from Sanskrit to Newari, the language of the Newar people in the Kathmandu Valley, and kings gradually shifted from Buddhism to Hinduism. Politically, leading notables with names ending in *malla* ("wrestler" in Sanskrit) became prominent in the early twelfth century. The most renowned Malla ruler was Yakshamalla, who ruled from 1428 to 1482. He both ended elite power struggles in the Kathmandu Valley and extended his influence outside the region.

After Yakshamalla's death, the Malla kingdom became divided among his descendents into three competing kingdoms based in Bhadgaon, Kathmandu, and Patan. The three-kingdoms period lasted until the mid-eighteenth century and was characterized by repeated warfare among the kingdoms over ritual slights and miniscule territorial gains. States outside the Kathmandu Valley fought each other and engaged in various, shifting alliances with Malla kingdoms. Malla rulers continued to legitimize their rule as protectors of dharma, and the Kathmandu Valley's unique culture blossomed as temples and palace complexes were constructed, many of which still exist. As the Mughal Dynasty (1526–1858) expanded throughout South Asia, dispossessed Indian princes found shelter in Nepal's hilly regions and brought the Khasa language, which evolved into the present Nepali language. They also brought Mughal military goods, such as firearms and artillery, and administrative techniques, such as providing land in return for military service.

The Making of Modern Nepal: Founded in 1559, Gorkha was among the hill states that struggled for power during the later Malla period, sometimes allying with one or more of the three kingdoms in their battles against each other. Gorkha achieved no notable territorial expansion until the rule of Prithvi Narayan Shah (1743–75), when the Nepalese state was established. An astute military strategist, Shah obtained financial assistance and armaments from India and then created alliances with neighboring states or purchased their neutrality. In fact, his forces even managed to repel British troops. On September 29, 1768, Gorkha troops entered Kathmandu during religious celebrations and took it without a fight. Shah defeated all three Malla kingdoms by 1769 and continued his conquests, conquering eastern Nepal by 1773.

Shah died in 1775. In the following decades, his heirs neglected issues of national administration and engaged in factional power struggles. Internal administration and foreign affairs were under the charge of the *mukhtiyar*, or prime minister, and the earliest *mukhtiyars* attempted to increase their own power by creating rifts among royal family members or by collaborating with some royal family members to liquidate enemies. As powerful families fought for power, Nepal's political and economic development suffered tremendously. To avoid military interference in court affairs, the military was granted the autonomy to pursue ever-larger conquests, and in turn the military became a powerful influence in domestic affairs.

Rana Rule: Intrigue and infighting among royal competitors continued until 1846, when Jang Bahadur Kunwar, a military commander, established a dynasty of prime ministers that would rule until 1951. The Rana dynasty essentially became a parallel monarchy in which the preeminent authority was the prime minister, a hereditary position with unclear rules of succession. The de jure monarchy was reduced to a ceremonial position that legitimized Rana rule with occasional decrees of support, and monarchs were either exiled or kept under house arrest. Rampant nepotism and inefficient administration handicapped political development, and rural development suffered from the delegation of authority to local kings and landlords who acted as autonomous dictators. The Ranas provided some positive development, such as eliminating slavery, establishing schools and factories, and consolidating independence through pragmatic foreign relations, particularly with China and Britain. Yet, Nepal also had archaic health, transportation, and economic infrastructures and rampant poverty.

Although most Nepalis had little reason to support Rana rule, the dynasty's end was largely precipitated by developments outside the country. Since the 1920s, Nepalis in India had published newspapers, formed political parties, and engaged in other activities challenging Rana rule. In the late 1940s, the British began their withdrawal from India and reduced their suppression of Nepali political groups, which took advantage of this opportunity to increase the scope and intensity of their activities, as well as their level of organization, particularly when the Nepali Congress party was formed in January 1947. The end of British rule in India in 1947 and the communist revolution in China in 1949 ended crucial foreign support for the Ranas, and India's new government wanted democratic government in Nepal. By November 1950, Nepalese rebels operating from India engaged Rana troops in the Tarai Region, and such activities were often supported by protests in Nepal. These mounting challenges eventually rendered the maintenance of power overly costly for the Ranas. On January 8, 1951, the last Rana oligarch, Mohan Shamsher, agreed to restore the king to power and hold elections. In February 1951, King Tribhuvan (r. 1911–55) returned to power.

The Democratic Experiment: From February 1951 to February 1959, numerous short-lived governments ruled either under an interim constitution or under the command of King Tribhuvan and his successor, Mahendra (r. 1955–72). The kings regularly dismissed uncooperative or poorly functioning ministries and continually postponed elections. However, after substantial popular protests, the king allowed the first national elections on February 18, 1959. The Nepali Congress won. But the king dismissed this government on December 15, 1960, and instituted a *panchayat* (village council) government, a four-tiered system of representative government with traditional village-level councils at the local level and the National Panchayat at the national level. The system ostensibly was responsive to local needs and input, but local councils had little effective power and often served as sources of patronage for the king, who continued to retain both absolute authority and support from the military.

King Mahendra died in January 1972, and his successor, Birendra (r. 1972–2001), adopted a more liberal approach to government. In May 1980, for example, King Birendra held a national referendum on the *panchayat* system, and he interpreted the narrow margin of support (54.7 percent voted in favor) as a need for political change. His government soon allowed direct elections to the National Panchayat, and in May 1981 Surya Bahadar Thapa was elected prime minister. In 1983 Thapa's government fell as a result of corruption charges and a food crisis, and Lokendra Bahadur Chand became prime minister. However, factional tensions between supporters of Thapa and Chand nearly paralyzed the National Panchayat, and in the second general election in 1986, Marich Man Singh Shrestha was elected prime minister. The Nepali Congress boycotted the election, but it and other parties were widely regarded as having substantially declined in effectiveness.

In the 1980s, Nepal once again underwent tumultuous change. Nepal's improving relations with China placed stress on its relations with India, and for this and other reasons India terminated trade and transit treaties in March 1989. The loss of trade routes and exports essentially devastated Nepal's economy, which was already straining under falling agricultural production, increasing factory layoffs, and growing inflation. Political parties campaigned for the end of the *panchayat* system, and after a period of strikes and violent demonstrations, foreign nations pressured King Birendra to allow democratic reforms.

On April 18, 1990, King Birendra invited K.P. Bhattarai, president of the Nepali Congress, to form a government, and Bhattarai subsequently headed a cabinet composed of representatives of political parties and human rights groups as well as two royal appointees. After months of contentious negotiations between the king and the new cabinet, a new constitution was promulgated on November 9, 1990, with provisions for basic human rights, adult franchise, and a multiparty democracy with the king as a constitutional monarch. The cabinet and political parties reportedly feared that the king could misuse some provisions in the constitution, but they accepted it as the best document possible under the tense circumstances in which it was drafted. Elections were held in May 1991, and K.P. Bhattarai and the Nepali Congress came to power.

The restoration of democracy initially brought tremendous optimism that Nepal would experience improvements in various spheres of life, but by the end of the 1990s various developments culminated to make the era one of the most difficult in the country's history, threatening its very existence. The earlier trade and transit impasse with India was quickly settled, but other economic problems worsened, sometimes to near-crisis levels. High inflation and substantial foreign debt limited the government's capacity to address economic development and poverty alleviation. Furthermore, the open political climate enabled various social groups to express long-held ethnic and linguistic grievances and to demand policy changes. Perhaps most importantly, a civil conflict began in February 1996 in which the Communist Party of Nepal (Maoist) killed, expelled, and threatened government officials, landlords, and others it charged with economic and political oppression of Nepalis. Initially, the government largely ignored the conflict, but by 2000 the conflict had expanded to nearly two-thirds of the country.

Furthermore, unstable political institutions and worsening civil conflict weakened the government's capacity to address economic, social, and other problems. Factional fighting within and among political parties led to rapid changes in government and prompted parties to spend precious time and resources on maintaining or acquiring power. In 1994 the Nepali Congress was defeated in midterm elections, and the Communist Party of Nepal (Unified Marxist-Leninist) formed a minority government that lasted nine months. A coalition government led by the Nepali Congress came into power in September 1995 with Sher Bahadur Deuba as prime minister. This coalition remained in power until 2002, but contentious relations with opposition parties and within the coalition often undermined the coalition's stability and diverted attention from worsening social and economic problems.

Events since 2000 suggest that Nepal may once again experience drastic change. In one of the most remarkable events in Nepal's history, Crown Prince Dipendra killed the king, queen, and other royal family members on June 1, 2001, reportedly over his choice of a bride. The crown passed to Gyanendra (r. 2001–), Dipendra's uncle, who adopted a relatively firmer approach to political issues. When cease-fire talks with the Maoists ended in November 2001, King Gyanendra declared a state of emergency and sent the army into the conflict. This action had the unintended effect of intensifying the conflict. When most political parties were unwilling to extend the state of emergency, Prime Minister Deuba requested and received the dissolution of parliament by the king in May 2002. In October 2002, the king unconstitutionally released Deuba's government and assumed executive powers. After two successive prime ministers resigned, the king reinstated Deuba as prime minister but then dismissed Deuba's government and suspended the constitution in February 2005, citing the worsening civil conflict.

GEOGRAPHY

Location: Nepal is located in the Himalaya Mountains of South Asia, with India to the east, south, and west and China to the north.

Size: Nepal's total land area is 147,181 square kilometers.

Land Boundaries: Nepal's northern boundary (1,236 kilometers in length) is shared with China, and the other borders (1,690 kilometers) are shared with India.

Click to Enlarge Image

Disputed Territory: Nepal and China have no territorial disputes, but Nepal and India have several: possession of a 75-square-kilometer area called Kalapani, which is further complicated by its proximity to the Chinese border; the boundary of the Maha Kali River (Sarda River in India), with ramifications for development and distribution of hydropower and water resources; possession of 209 hectares of land after changes in the course of the Mechi River; and sovereignty over several areas comprising nearly 600 square kilometers along the border.

Length of Coastline: None. Nepal is landlocked.

Topography: Mountains and rugged hills cover nearly 75 percent of Nepal's land area. The landscape is composed of three main physiographic regions that run laterally across the country. In the south, the plains of the Tarai Region cover approximately 23 percent of Nepal's total area and are both the main agricultural region and the most densely populated region. To the north, the Hill Region covers approximately 42 percent of the total area and consists of mountains, hills, flatlands, and valleys with elevations ranging from 600 to 3,000 meters. Farther north, the Himalayan Region covers nearly 35 percent of the total area and contains 200 peaks more than 6,000 meters in elevation and 13 peaks more than 8,000 meters high, including Sagarmatha (Mount Everest), the world's highest mountain (8,850 meters). This area often experiences intense geological activity, with nearly 50 earthquakes from 1870 to 1996.

Principal Rivers: Nepal's three major river systems are—from east to west—the Kosi (513 kilometers), Narayani (332 kilometers), and Karnali (507 kilometers). All are major tributaries of the Ganga in northern India.

Climate: Nepal lies within a subtropical monsoon climate zone. Climatic conditions and precipitation tend to vary with elevation, ranging from tropical in the Tarai plains to alpine and tundra in the northern mountain areas. Temperatures range from 5° C to 47° C in the Tarai Region, from 0° to 28° C in the Hill Region, and from below 0° C to 16° C in the Himalayas. Annual rainfall generally increases with elevation up to 3,000 meters, thereafter declining with elevation and latitude. Precipitation tends to be highest in the east and declines westward, but certain areas in central Nepal have consistently high rainfall. The majority of precipitation— nearly 80 percent—occurs during the annual monsoon. The pre-monsoon season from March to May is hot and dry, the monsoon season (generally June to September) is hot, and the post-monsoon season typically lasts through mid-October. Mid-October through March is typically dry and cold.

Natural Resources: Nepal's natural resource base is widely regarded as insufficient for economic needs, and "scenic beauty" is seen as one of the most commercially important resources. Fuel resources are especially scarce. Although some methane gas has been discovered, petroleum reserves have not materialized. Renewable resources, particularly arable land, are perhaps the most economically important resources, but hydropower is underutilized. The most available metallic minerals are copper, gold, lead, and zinc, but only lead and zinc have been commercially viable. Nonmetallic minerals such as marble, talc, and particularly limestone have been commercially viable, and there are some deposits of dolomite and magnesite.

Land Use: Nepal's mountainous terrain constrains land use options, and nearly one-third of the land area is unfit for agriculture or forestry. According to government figures for 2002, approximately 18 percent of the total land area was used for agriculture, of which 88.8 percent was categorized as arable land, 4.4 percent as land under permanent crops, and the remainder as pastures, woodlands, and other categories. Most agricultural land is in the Hill and Tarai regions. From 1962 to 2002, the total area of arable land increased (from 1.6 million to 2.5 million hectares) but declined as a proportion of land for agriculture (from 94.5 to 88.8 percent) because of the increase in land used for grazing and permanent crops, particularly fruit. Permanent crop cultivation also has reduced the proportion of land used for woodland and forest harvesting.

Environmental Factors: Nepal has numerous environmental problems. Sedimentation and discharge of industrial effluents are prominent sources of water pollution, and fuelwood burning is a significant source of indoor air pollution and respiratory problems. Vehicular and industrial emissions increasingly have contributed to air pollution in urban areas. Deforestation and land degradation appear to affect a far greater proportion of the population and have the worst consequences for economic growth and individuals' livelihoods. Forest loss has contributed to floods, soil erosion, and stagnant agricultural output. Estimates suggest that from 1966 to 2000 forest cover declined from 45 to 29 percent of the total land area. Often cited causes of deforestation include population growth, high fuelwood consumption, infrastructure projects, and conversion of forests into grazing- and cropland. According to government estimates, 1.5 million tons of soil nutrients are lost annually, and by 2002 approximately 5 percent of agricultural holdings had been rendered uncultivable as a result of soil erosion and flooding. Land degradation is attributed to population growth, improper use of agro-chemicals, and overly intensive use of landholdings that are too small to provide most households with sufficient food. Since the late 1980s, government policies have attempted to address these numerous and related problems, but policies often are hampered by lack of funding, insufficient understanding of Nepal's mountain ecosystems, bureaucratic inefficiency, and sometimes contentious relations between the central government and local communities.

Time Zone: Nepal is 5:45 hours ahead of Greenwich Mean Time (GMT) and does not observe daylight saving time.

SOCIETY

Population: From 1911 to 2001, the country's total population grew from an estimated 5.6 million to 23.2 million inhabitants. However, Nepal's census figures do not include approximately 102,892 refugees from Bhutan (United Nations estimate for 2003), most of whom are from Nepalese ethnic groups. The population growth rate averaged 2 percent annually from 1911 to 2001 but has often been higher than 2 percent since the 1960s. From 1911 to 2001, population density grew from 38.3 to 157.3 persons per square kilometer. In 2001 population density ranged from fewer than 5 persons per square kilometer in some Himalayan areas to 2,738.9 persons per square kilometer in Kathmandu. Population size, density, and growth rates tend to be highest in districts bordering India and in districts around Kathmandu. In 2001, 84.1 percent of the population lived in rural areas and 14.2 percent in urban areas.

Demography: According to the 2001 census, 50.1 percent of the population was male and 49.9 percent female, a proportion that has existed for decades. Furthermore, 39.4 percent of the population was less than 15 years of age, 54.1 percent was 15 to 59 years of age, and 6.5 percent was 60 years of age or older. Thus, for every 100 persons of working age, there were 84.7 dependents—one of the world's highest "dependency ratios." Life expectancy at birth was 60.1 years for males, 60.7 years for females, or 60.4 overall. According to census figures for 1961 to 2001, the crude birthrate fell from 47 to 30.5 births per 1,000 persons, the crude death rate fell from 22 to 10.8 deaths per 1,000 persons, the total fertility rate fell from 5.7 to 3.8 children born per woman, and the infant mortality rate fell from approximately 190 to 64.4 deaths under one year of age per 1,000 live births.

Ethnic Groups: Analysis of Nepal's ethnic groups is complicated by the sensitive nature of ethnic and linguistic identity and the fact that no anthropological or linguistic survey of the population has ever been conducted. The names of ethnic groups often are derived from the language they speak, and ethnic identity is based on various combinations of national origin, region, language, religion, and caste. The broadest classification of ethnicity is national origin, which includes three major groups: Indo-Nepalese, who originated in India; Tibeto-Nepalese, who are of Tibeto-Mongol origin; and indigenous Nepalese, whose habitation predates the other groups. Nepal's census provides more specific ethnic classifications, including more than 100 ethnic and caste groups that are classified into five larger groups on the basis of shared and prominent cultural traits: Hindus (59 percent of the population), indigenous Janajatis (31 percent), Newars (5.5 percent), Muslims (4.3 percent), and others, a category that includes Sikhs, Bengalis, Marwaris, and Jains (0.2 percent). The government acknowledges, however, that these categorizations are provisional and arbitrary. Ethnic differences often have complicated national integration and unification, especially after democratic reforms in the early 1990s reduced risks of cultural expression for minority groups. Although ethnic issues have not been as prominent or contentious as elsewhere in South Asia, various groups have mobilized to address perceived traditional political and economic domination by other groups.

Languages: Nepal's 2001 census listed 92 languages spoken as mother tongues, and an indeterminate number of languages were categorized as "unknown." Many languages are rarely spoken outside of specific areas, but knowledge of more than one language is common. Nepali is the national language and the most common mother tongue (spoken by 48.6 percent of the population), as well as the most common second language. Maithili is the second most common mother tongue (12.3 percent), and English is increasingly prominent as well as compulsory in public schools and universities. With the end of the government's "one-nation-one language" policy in 1991, the percentage of people reporting Nepali as their mother tongue has declined, and language has grown as a marker of social identification and social division.

Religion: Nepal is the world's only constitutionally declared Hindu state, and the constitution protects religious and cultural freedom. According to the 2001 census, 80.6 percent of Nepalese are Hindu, 10.7 percent are Buddhist, 4.2 are Muslim, 3.6 percent are Kirat (an indigenous religion), 0.5 percent are Christian, and 0.4 percent are classified as other groups. Although the population is mostly Hindu, since the 1971 census Hindus have shown the greatest decline as a proportion of the population, and Buddhists and Kirats have increased the most: in 1971 Hindus were 89.4 percent of the population, Buddhists 7.5 percent, and Kirats statistically 0 percent. However, statistics on religious groups are complicated by the ubiquity of dual faith practices—particularly among Hindus and Buddhists. Moreover, shifts in the population's religious composition also reflect political changes. The 1990 constitution ended the government's promotion of Hindu nationalism and official suppression of political participation based on religious, cultural, and linguistic traits. This policy has enabled greater freedom of religious expression and allowed the census to officially enumerate more religious groups.

Education and Literacy: Education and literacy statistics have improved, but economic and cultural issues complicate the pursuit of education for many Nepalese. High poverty rates, particularly in rural areas, present numerous obstacles. The government provides tuition-free education to all children between the ages of six and 12, yet families often lack sufficient funds to cover non-tuition costs, such as books and clothing. Similarly, poor families often need their children to work. As a result, many children start school at a late age, such as nine or 10, and dropout rates are high. Education is not compulsory, and only 49.7 percent of students completed the fourth grade in 1999. However, from 1996 to 2004 the percentage of the population that had ever attended school increased from 34 percent to 46 percent, and from 1981 to 2001 the adult literacy rate increased from 20.6 percent to 48.6 percent. Another barrier to education is a common perception that there is little value in educating females. Still, gender disparities in education have declined. From 1990 to 2004, the percentage of female students at the "school" level (grades one to 10) increased from nearly 30 percent to 45.9 percent.

As for educational infrastructure, in 2004 Nepal had 26,277 schools; 6,018,806 students; and 147,677 teachers, 32.9 percent of whom had formal training. Basic education consists of three levels: primary (grades one to five), lower secondary (grades six to eight), and secondary (grades nine and 10). In 1989 higher secondary schools were introduced for higher education preparation, and by 2003 there were 789 such schools. Institutions of higher education included eight public and 114 private technical schools, one polytechnic school, and six universities in 2001. The overall number of education facilities has grown, but most are in urban areas. Moreover, most funding is for primary education. For example, 55.4 percent of the 2003 education budget was for primary education. From 1990 to 2003, the share of the government budget allocated to education increased from 9.1 percent to 15.8 percent, and government-funded schools accounted for more than 85 percent of enrollment. However, private schools are often seen as offering higher-quality education.

Health: Health indicators are poor by international standards, especially in rural areas, but suggest some improvements. Disease prevalence is higher than in other South Asian countries. Leading diseases and illnesses include diarrhea, gastrointestinal disorders, goiter, intestinal parasites, leprosy, and tuberculosis. Nepal also has high rates of child malnutrition (72 percent in 2001) and under-five mortality (91.2 deaths per 1,000 live births in 2001). According to United Nations data for 2003, approximately 60,000 persons aged 15 to 49 had human immunodeficiency virus (HIV), and the HIV prevalence rate was 0.5 percent. In spite of these figures, evidence suggests some improvement. For example, Nepal's Human Development Index (HDI) was 0.504 in 2002, ranking Nepal 140 out of 177 countries, up from 0.291 in 1975.

Health-care facilities, hygiene, nutrition, and sanitation generally are poor and beyond the means of most, particularly in rural areas. Provision of health services is constrained by low government spending, rugged terrain, and lack of health education (which lowers the demand for health services). Most hospitals are located in urban areas, and rural health facilities often lack adequate funding, trained staff, and medicines. Thus, health clinics and hospitals generally are used only for persistent and serious illnesses. The government has tried decentralizing health services to villages, but the program has not provided notable public health improvements. In 2003 Nepal had 10 health centers, 83 hospitals, 700 health posts, and 3,158 "sub-health posts," which serve villages. In addition, there were 1,259 physicians, or one physician for every 18,400 persons. In 2000 government funding for health matters was approximately US$2.30 per person, and approximately 70 percent of health expenditures came from out-of-pocket contributions. Government allocations for health were around 5.1 percent of the budget for fiscal year 2004, and foreign donors provided around 30 percent of the total budget for health expenditures.

Welfare: The government has made progress in road construction, communications, literacy rates, and health services. Most of these developments, however, have occurred in urban areas, while rural areas—where most of the population lives—often lack basic amenities such as drinking water, health services, and transportation facilities. Nongovernmental organizations and foreign aid providers are important sources of development funds. Domestic agencies in charge of development projects have been criticized as poorly organized and often ineffective.

ECONOMY

Overview: According to the 1990 constitution, the government has a fundamental economic responsibility to create an independent and self-reliant economy through equitable distribution of economic resources and gains, prevention of economic exploitation, and the advancement of private and public enterprise. However, according to observers, such changes require economic reforms that have yet to materialize. Prior to 1990, the economy, like the country, was essentially closed to the world, and international economic relations were largely in the form of cross-border trade with India and China. Since 1990, the government increasingly has adopted market-oriented policies with greater liberalization of the domestic economy and trade. These policies have focused on privatizing state industries and creating joint-venture projects, particularly in financial institutions. Liberalization policies, however, have been criticized for benefiting primarily urban areas and rural elites. The economy is still characterized by central planning. Indeed, the government is the main source of domestic investment, and five-year plans direct such investment. However, five-year economic development plans alternately emphasize various sectors, and as a result, development has been uneven.

The economy has been—and continues to be—characterized by dependence on agricultural output, a poor export base but strong reliance on trade, unbalanced regional development, dependence on foreign aid, excessive government control and regulation, and inefficient public enterprises and administration. The agricultural sector has employed most of the labor force and provided the largest share of gross domestic product (GDP), but the sector's shares of the labor force and GDP have declined since the 1970s. Industry and manufacturing have provided lower portions of GDP, employed fewer people, and expanded little. Services, particularly those related to tourism, have grown in importance, but the civil conflict has hurt this and other sectors.

Gross Domestic Product (GDP)/Power Purchasing Parity (PPP): World Bank and Nepal government data indicate that from 1960 to 2004 total GDP grew from US$1.4 billion to US$6.2 billion, averaging 3.6 percent annual growth for the period. From 1960 to 2000, GDP per capita increased from US$139 to US$240; it was US$271 in 2004. From 1975 to 2004, PPP per capita grew from US$344 to nearly US$1,470. In terms of sectoral composition, World Bank data suggest that from 1965 to 2004 the agricultural sector decreased from 65.5 percent to 40.3 percent of GDP (37 percent in 2004 according to the Nepal government), while services increased from 23.5 percent to 36.7 percent of GDP (38.7 percent according to the government), manufacturing from 3.3 percent to 9 percent (7.4 percent according to the government), and industry from 7.7 percent to 14 percent (12.6 percent according to the government). Since the intensification of civil conflict in 2002, projections of GDP growth often have hinged on forecasts of the security situation.

10

Government Budget: The Ministry of Finance and the National Planning Commission establish the budget with guidance from five-year plans drafted by the National Development Council. In July 2004, the government reclassified budget categories from regular and development expenditures to current expenditures for administration and security matters, capital expenditures on programs and projects for production and output, and loan repayment expenditures. From 1972 to 2004, total expenditures grew from US$879 million to US$1.2 billion and were estimated to be US$1.4 billion in fiscal year (FY) 2005. Current expenditures were 61.5 percent of total expenditures in FY2004 (US$746 million), with most allocated to social services (37.5 percent), general administration (13.2 percent), and defense (11.9 percent). Capital expenditures constituted 26.5 percent of total expenditures in FY2004 (US$310 million), with most allocated to economic services (56.8 percent) and social services (30.9 percent). Finally, since FY1999 repayment expenditures have doubled, amounting to 12 percent of total expenditures in FY2004 (US$145 million), with 53.4 percent for external loans and 46.6 percent for internal loans.

From 1972 to 2000, fiscal deficits increased from US$125 million to US$12 billion but declined to US$208 million by FY2004. Moreover, the first quarter of FY2005 showed a budget surplus of US$42.7 million. These changes are largely due to substantial increases in government revenues and foreign grants. Public-sector funds traditionally have suffered from a narrow tax base and numerous tax exemptions, but government revenues have increased as a result of improvements in revenue administration and governance. In FY2004, government revenues totaled US$837.8 million—77.3 percent tax revenue and 22.7 percent non-tax revenue.

Inflation: According to World Bank figures, inflation averaged nearly 9 percent from 1965 to 2000. From 2000 to 2004, inflation declined to between 4 and 5 percent. According to Nepal's central bank, from 2000 to 2004 the consumer price index ranged from 2.5 to 5.7 percent and averaged 4.5 percent for fiscal year 2005.

Agriculture, Forestry, and Fishing: Agriculture is probably Nepal's most important economic sector. According to available data, since at least the 1960s this sector has often provided nearly half of the gross domestic product (GDP) and employed most of the population. However, the sector's contribution to the economy has declined. According to World Bank data, from 1965 to 2004 the agricultural sector declined from 65.5 percent of GDP to nearly 40.3 percent. Moreover, the percentage of the labor force employed in agriculture fell from 94.4 percent in 1971 to approximately 65.7 percent in 2001. Forestry and fishing often are categorized as agriculture in government statistics, and each accounts for less than 1 percent of GDP and the labor force.

As a result of low agricultural growth rates and high population growth rates, Nepal has not been self-sufficient in food grain production since the 1980s. Low growth rates generally are seen as a result of limited use of agricultural technologies and declining landholding sizes. From 1962 to 2002, the total agricultural area increased about 57 percent, and the number of landholdings grew approximately 120 percent, but the population increased by 146 percent. In the same period, the amount of agricultural land declined from 0.18 to 0.13 hectares per person, and the average size of holdings has declined from 1.1 to 0.8 hectares. In 2002 nearly 60 percent of holdings did not produce sufficient food to feed a household, and almost 97 percent of these holdings were two hectares in size or smaller. Furthermore, tractors or threshers are used on less than 10 percent of total holdings, and approximately 65 percent of landholdings are rain-fed rather than irrigated.

The use of pesticides, fertilizers, high-yielding seeds, and irrigation has increased but mostly by owners of landholdings larger than two hectares. Cropping intensity has increased, with adverse environmental consequences, such as soil erosion.

Mining and Minerals: This sector has traditionally been one of Nepal's weakest. Most minerals are used domestically, often for construction. The value of mining and quarrying output increased from US$15.3 million in 1990 to an estimated US$31.1 million in 2004. The percentage of the labor force employed in mining and quarrying increased from statistically 0 percent in 1971 to 0.2 percent in 2001. Despite these increases, the sector remained at 0.5 percent of gross domestic product from 1990 to 2004. Furthermore, mining of all metallic minerals has declined with the exception of small alluvial deposits of gold accessed during short periods of time when river levels are low. The sector's decline reflects the lack of commercial viability for most minerals as a result of the high costs of accessing and marketing minerals in Nepal. Mineral deposits are often small, scattered, and in areas far from domestic markets, and transportation is generally inadequate and relies on costly, imported fuels.

Industry and Manufacturing: Industry and manufacturing have grown but lag behind other economic sectors. Indeed, observers often contend that Nepal's industrial and trade policies require further reforms if this sector is to grow. Manufacturing is often regarded as sluggish in both output and growth, and the limited industrial base relies on agricultural products and imported inputs, particularly from India. In fact, most industrial output is provided by traditional cottage industries such as basket-weaving and cotton fabric production. Most large plants are in the public sector and produce items such as jute, sugar, cigarettes, and chemicals. Smaller industries generally process minerals, which are often consumed domestically. From 1965 to 2004, manufacturing grew from 3.3 percent of gross domestic product (GDP) to approximately 9 percent, and industry grew from 7.7 percent of GDP to approximately 14 percent. From 1971 to 2001, the percentage of the labor force employed in manufacturing increased from 1.1 percent to 8.8 percent, and the percentage employed in industries other than manufacturing increased from 0.1 percent to 4.5 percent.

Energy: Most energy is derived from traditional sources, particularly fuelwood. However, traditional fuel consumption has fallen as a percentage of total energy requirements, from nearly 95 percent in the 1980s to an estimated 88 percent in 2001. Nepal relies heavily on hydropower, but its tremendous potential for increasing hydroelectric output is limited by difficult terrain, lack of infrastructure, insufficient capital investment, and civil conflict. According to the World Bank, commercial energy production has consistently lagged behind commercial energy use, and the gap appears to be growing. From 1971 to 1999, commercial energy production increased from 2,506 kilotons of oil equivalent to 7,035 kilotons, and commercial energy use increased from 2,570 kilotons of oil equivalent to 8,051 kilotons. In the same period, the amount of commercial energy that was imported increased from 2.5 percent to 12.6 percent. Finally, from 1971 to 2001 the percentage of the labor force employed in "electricity, gas, and water" increased from 0.04 percent to 1.5 percent.

Services: Services grew from 23.5 percent of gross domestic product in 1965 to 36.7 percent in 2004. Average annual growth in services was 4.9 percent from 1965 to 2000 but 6.2 percent in the 1990s. Furthermore, the percentage of the labor force employed in the services sector increased substantially, from 4.4 percent in 1971 to 18.3 percent in 2001. No particular industry accounts for a great percentage of the overall services sector's total value. Indeed, in 2004 the total value of the services sector was nearly evenly divided among finance and real estate (27 percent); trade, restaurants, and hotels (25.8 percent); community and social services (24.3 percent); and transportation, communication, and storage (22.8 percent).

Banking and Finance: The central bank, the Nepal Rastra Bank (NRB), has authority over the banking system, development capital mobilization, and monetary policy. However, its capacity to perform these functions was not independent of the state's commercial interests until the bank gained autonomy from the Ministry of Finance in 2002. From 1960 to 2004, the NRB's total assets grew from US$11.2 million to US$4.2 billion. In July 2004, nonperforming assets were 28.8 percent of total assets. In 2005 Nepal had 17 commercial banks with 382 branches, 18 insurance companies, 20 financial cooperatives, 59 finance companies, and 25 development banks, with 11 offering microcredit services; 47 nongovernmental organizations were licensed to be intermediaries for microcredit services. However, civil conflict has reduced banking and financial providers in some rural areas. As of July 2005, 128 companies were listed on the Nepal Stock Exchange.

The government's strong influence over many major financial institutions is often cited as a major reason for the sector's poor performance, but the World Bank contends that recent reforms have yielded improvements. In 2001 foreign banks were permitted to have majority ownership in joint ventures, but foreign investment has been low because of security and other concerns. In 2005 the government banned many loan defaulters from employment in government ministries, yet because royal family members and high-level politicians were among the defaulters, questions were raised about this directive's implementation. Moreover, the government has major shareholdings in the two largest commercial banks, which possess 50 percent of total banking assets and thus provide the state a near monopoly on credit. Like many major financial institutions in Nepal, these banks have operated at a loss for years. In 2003 their nonperforming loans were more than 50 percent of loans, which was an improvement over previous years. Subsequent restructuring has had some positive results, and, for example, the two aforementioned banks earned net profits in 2004.

Tourism: Tourism is an important component of the economy, but although the government has undertaken various measures to increase tourism, the deteriorating security situation has hurt the industry. Since the early 1990s, the government has abolished travel restrictions in some remote areas, constructed numerous tourist centers, and allowed access to an additional 103 mountains (a total of 263 mountains can be accessed). Tourist expenditures grew from US$43.2 million in 1980 to US$162.4 million in 2001, declined sharply to US$102.3 million in 2002 but recovered to US$166.8 million in 2004. Similarly, the number of tourist arrivals increased from 163,000 in 1980 to 492,000 in 1999 but declined to 288,356 in 2004. From January to June 2005, tourist arrivals were 25 percent lower than for the same period in 2004.

Labor: In 2001, 58.2 percent of the population age 10 and older was economically active. Officially, 2 percent of the population was unemployed, and 4 percent of the employed were involuntarily underemployed. According to the government's statistics, most persons aged 15 years and older in 1999 were employed in the agricultural sector (65.7 percent), followed by commerce (9.9 percent), manufacturing (8.8 percent), personal and community services (6.7 percent), construction (2.9 percent), and tourism (2 percent). In addition, government figures suggest the informal sector accounts for 73 percent of employment in "main jobs" outside the agricultural sector.

Labor regulations and conditions have shown mixed signs since the early 1990s. Since the establishment of democracy in 1991, the government has passed several labor laws. Limitations on labor unions have been reduced, and union publications suggest slight improvements in labor practices and worker treatment. However, problems such as child and bonded labor persist. In 1999 nearly 21 percent of children five to nine years old were in the labor force, as were nearly 61 percent of children 10 to 14 years old. This situation may change as a result of a 1999 ordinance banning employment of persons less than 14 years of age, and since 2000 the government has outlawed human trafficking, forbidden a prominent form of bonded labor (*kamaiya*), and increased the number of countries in which Nepalese could legally seek employment (from 25 to 108). However, enforcement and implementation of labor laws are weak. For example, many labor restrictions do not apply to businesses that are unregistered or that have 10 or fewer employees, and many Nepalese work in the unregulated informal sector.

Foreign Economic Relations: The country's landlocked position and mountainous terrain limit trade to cross-border traffic, and most goods come either from or through India. Trade relations with India are occasionally contentious, and Nepalese policymakers have argued that Nepal's ability to independently create and implement economic policies is restricted by the long and open border with India and dependence on Indian export markets. Since the late 1980s, trade disputes with India have exacerbated a perpetual trade deficit and reduced Nepalese exports to India. Nepal gained member status with the World Trade Organization on April 23, 2004.

Imports: Nepal's imports of goods and services (in current U.S. dollars) grew steadily from US$102.4 million in 1965 to US$1.8 billion in 2004, and increases in oil costs have been a major contributor to growth in imports. From 1965 to 2004, imports of goods and services increased as a percentage of gross domestic product from 13.9 percent to 31.7 percent, averaging 20.7 percent for the 1965–2004 period. Major imports include petroleum products, textiles, vehicles, fertilizer, crude palm oil, and machinery. More than 50 percent of imports come from India, and other important sources of imports are Singapore, China, Malaysia, and Indonesia.

Exports: Exports of goods and services (in current U.S. dollars) grew from US$57.1 million in 1965 to US$712 million in 2004 and increased as a percentage of gross domestic product from 7.8 percent to 16.8 percent, averaging 13.2 percent for the period. Major exports include garments, carpets, grain, vegetable oil (ghee), pashmina wool, jute goods, and leather goods. Approximately 50 percent of exports go to India, and other important export markets are the United States and Germany.

Trade Balance: According to the World Bank and Nepal's central bank, Nepal has had a trade deficit every year since 1965. From 1965 to 2004, the trade deficit grew from US$45.3 million— about 6 percent of gross domestic product (GDP)—to about US$1.1 billion—nearly 18 percent of GDP.

Balance of Payments: According to World Bank and Nepal government figures, Nepal had a current account deficit every year from 1977 to 2003. Current account deficits averaged US$153.5 million in the 1980s and US$327 million in the 1990s. However, in fiscal year (FY) 2004, the current account had a surplus of US$197.3 million and also is expected to post a surplus in FY2005, although lower than in FY2004. The improvement is largely attributed to lower trade deficits and increased remittances from Nepalese working in foreign countries.

External Debt: Government debt has grown substantially since at least the 1970s. According to the World Bank, central government debt was 5.9 percent of gross domestic product in 1975, 66.2 percent in 1995, and 51.8 percent in 2004. In dollar amounts, external debt was US$33.7 million in 1975, US$2.4 billion in 1995, and US$3.5 billion in 2004. According to Nepal's Ministry of Finance, outstanding foreign loans totaled US$3.2 billion in 2004.

Foreign Investment: Foreign direct investment (FDI) commenced in the 1980s and has fluctuated tremendously. FDI increased from US$7 million in 1996 to US$28.4 million in 1997, declined to US$3.4 million by 2000, and then increased to US$35 million in 2004. In 2004 the greatest proportion of FDI came from India, with 37 percent of total fixed capital investment, followed by the United States, with 16 percent of total investment. The government is eager to increase FDI, particularly in the energy and transportation sectors, but corruption, a large and slow bureaucracy, bank lending policies, the tax structure, and civil conflict have undercut investment appeal and made foreign companies cautious about investing in Nepal. Furthermore, journalists, academics, and others have criticized the concentration of investment in urban areas as exacerbating economic and infrastructural disparities between urban and rural areas.

Foreign Aid: Nepal relies heavily on foreign aid, and donors coordinate development aid policy through the Nepal Development Forum, whose members include donor countries, international financial institutions (such as the World Bank), and intergovernmental organizations (such as the United Nations). Japan is Nepal's largest bilateral aid donor, and the World Bank and Asian Development Bank are the largest multilateral donors. Donors have been reported as losing confidence in Nepal as a result of political interference and corruption in poverty relief efforts as well as the country's apparently poor capacity to utilize aid. According to World Bank figures, official development assistance increased from US$8.2 million in 1960 to US$369 million in 2003 and then fell to US$177 million in 2004. According to Nepal's Ministry of Finance, total foreign aid committed in fiscal year (FY) 2003 was US$555 million, with 63.3 percent in grants and 36.7 percent in loans. In FY2004, total foreign aid committed was US$320 million, of which 37.7 percent was grants and 62.3 percent, loans. In June 2004, active World Bank credits totaled US$302 million, with the greatest portions allocated to the financial sector (US$91.5 million) and to energy and mining (US$75.6 million).

Currency and Exchange Rate: The official currency is the Nepalese rupee (NPR). In early November 2005, the exchange rate was approximately NPR73=US$1. For domestic usage, the Nepalese rupee has a fixed exchange rate with the Indian rupee. The two currencies are freely convertible in Nepal but have different international exchange rates.

Fiscal Year: Nepal's fiscal year runs from July 16 through July 15.

TRANSPORTATION AND TELECOMMUNICATIONS

Overview: Nepal's transportation system is generally regarded as poor and an obstacle to economic development. The mountainous terrain physically constrains the development of the transportation network, and for decades the government has lacked sufficient funds to maintain, improve, and expand the transportation infrastructure, which has thus relied heavily on foreign funding. The transportation infrastructure is concentrated in the central and eastern parts of the Tarai Region and generally diminishes north and west of the Tarai. Nonmechanized transportation is common in both rural and urban areas, and mechanized local transportation is common only in the Kathmandu Valley and to a lesser degree in Pokhara. The major modes of transportation are air and road, and trails often are used to transport goods. Railroads are minimal and have declined in quality and quantity. The Department of Transport Management oversees transportation issues, and its fiscal year (FY) 2005 budget was approximately US$462,000 based on the official exchange rate for 2004. The FY2006 budget is nearly US$686,000.

Roads: Roads are Nepal's principal transportation mode. From 1951 to 2005, total road length increased from 376 kilometers to 17,217 kilometers, including 4,781 kilometers paved, 4,703 kilometers gravel-covered, and 7,643 kilometers classified as fair weather roads. The total road length also includes 3,028.7 kilometers of national highways. Roads are concentrated in the central and eastern regions, and the government is under pressure to expand and improve roads. Government allocations for roads have increased, but construction and maintenance costs are high because of the mountainous topography, monsoon rains, and occasional landslides. In March 2005, there were 459,224 registered vehicles, 63.5 percent of which were motorcycles.

Railroads: Nepal's railroad system is small, outdated, and declining in use and quality. The two rail lines link to railheads in India. Government-owned Nepal Railways Company (NRC) maintains a 53-kilometer narrow-gauge rail line, which is composed of two sections that operate separately. A 32-kilometer section runs between Jaynagar in India to Janakpur in Nepal, and a 21-kilometer portion goes from Janakpur to Bijalpura. The NRC manages a six-kilometer line from Raxaul, India, to Birganj. The Janakpur line is used largely for passengers and the Birganj line, for freight. The Birganj dry port was completed in 2000 but only became operational in 2005 because of the lack of an operating agreement between India and Nepal. From 1990 to 2000, passenger traffic ranged from 725,000 to 1.7 million per year and freight traffic, from 16 to 21 tons. The Janakpur railroad has lost money for years because of low fares, overstaffing, and political intervention, and the government has expressed interest in privatizing the NRC. In 2004 the government signed an agreement with the Container Corporation of India for container service between Birganj and various Indian cities, including Kokatta (Calcutta).

Ports: Nepal is a landlocked country with little waterway transportation and no waterway ports. However, the country has two inland container depots at Birganj and Sirsiya, which primarily service cargo to and from seaports in India. Both ports have experienced extended periods of nonuse because of problems such as customs disputes with India. There also have been proposals to use Janakpur as a dry port.

Inland and Coastal Waterways: Waterway transportation is virtually nonexistent because of the country's landlocked geographic position, mountainous topography, and deep gorges. The government has expressed interest in using waterways to connect exports with Indian markets, but feasibility studies have not been encouraging.

Civil Aviation and Airports: The government wants to expand civil aviation to overcome geographic constraints on transportation accessibility and to increase tourism. Civil aviation, however, has been slow to develop. In 2005 Nepal had 44 airports of varying standards—up from 43 in 1988—and only one international airport, Tribhuvan, located 5.6 kilometers east of Kathmandu. The number of international tourists arriving by air increased from 205,611 in 1987 to 421,243 in 1998 and then declined to 288,356 by 2004. Nepal has one government-owned airline (Royal Nepal Airlines Corporation), and 39 carriers provide international service. Sixteen carriers provide domestic cargo and passenger service. Air transportation is unavailable in 31 of Nepal's 75 districts.

Pipelines: Nepal has no pipelines. However, on September 9, 2004, the Nepal Oil Corporation signed a memorandum of understanding with the Indian Oil Corporation to build a 35-kilometer, pipeline from Raxaul (India) to Amalekhganj (Nepal) with an annual capacity of 1.1 million tons for transport of petroleum, diesel, and kerosene.

Telecommunications: Telecommunications generally have been poor in quality and are available mostly in Kathmandu. Nepal Telecommunications Corporation (NTC) had a monopoly on telecommunications services until various pieces of legislation since 1992 opened the NTC to privatization and allowed domestic and foreign companies to provide telecommunications services. The Nepal Telecommunications Authority (NTA) was established in 1998 to regulate and promote competition in the telecommunications sector. By 2005 there were 144 licensed telecommunications providers, and the number of fixed telephone lines increased from 65,000 in 1992 to 448,639. The waiting list for a telephone line is lengthy, only 3.1 of every 100 citizens had access to any type of telephone in 2003, and nearly 50 percent of village development areas did not have a single public phone. In July 2005, Nepal had 248,820 mobile telephone subscribers and approximately 225,000 Internet users. Legislation passed in 2004 was intended to address these matters, but the government suspended many mobile telephone and Internet services on February 1, 2005. From 1975 to 2001, the number of televisions per 1,000 people increased from 0 to 8, radios per 1,000 people increased from 17.5 to 39, and personal computers per 1,000 people increased from 0 to 3.5.

GOVERNMENT AND POLITICS

Government Overview: Nepal's constitution was promulgated on November 9, 1990, and is technically Nepal's fundamental law. The constitution guarantees certain rights to all citizens, protects individual liberties, and establishes Nepal as a "multiethnic, multilingual, democratic, independent, indivisible, sovereign, Hindu and Constitutional Monarchical Kingdom" with a parliamentary government and an independent judiciary. However King Gyanendra (r. 2001–) dissolved both houses of parliament in May 2002 as well as three subsequent interim governments composed of a prime minister and a Council of Ministers. The last interim government was suspended on February 1, 2005, and King Gyanendra has since ruled with full executive powers assisted by an appointed 10-person crisis cabinet. A state of emergency established by the king on February 1, 2005, was lifted on April 29, 2005, but civil rights and liberties remain restricted.

Since the restoration of democracy in 1990, the most prominent actors in Nepalese politics have been the king, the political parties, and the Maoist rebels. The single most powerful political entity is the king, who is the head of state, supreme commander of the Royal Nepal Army, and the constitutionally declared symbol of both the nation and national unity. The Raj Parishad, or King's Council, determines accession to the throne and the heir apparent, and the king appoints its members. The rule of kings has been culturally legitimized by the belief that kings are an incarnation of the Hindu god Vishnu and are upholders of dharma on earth, although it is debated how widely such beliefs are held. Royal power has been based on strong ties with the military and economic elites.

Executive Branch: Executive power is held by the king and the Council of Ministers, which is headed by the prime minister and consists of ministers appointed by the king on the prime minister's recommendation. Often referred to as His Majesty's Government of Nepal, the Council of Ministers is responsible for the general administration of the country as well as authenticating all transactions made in the king's name, except those in the king's exclusive domain. The Council of Ministers has a central secretariat consisting of 22 ministries and the secretariat of the National Planning Commission.

Legislative Branch: Nepal's legislature consists of the king and a bicameral parliament. The king's legislative powers are technically ceremonial, but the king approves or returns for reconsideration all bills approved by the two houses of parliament, except finance bills. The lower house of parliament, the House of Representatives (Pratindidhi Sabha), has authority over the Council of Ministers and is regarded as the more powerful of the two houses. The lower house has 205 members directly elected for five-year terms. The prime minister is the leader of the majority party and the country's chief executive. The upper house, the National Council (Rashtriya Sabha), has 60 members, who are appointed or indirectly elected to six-year terms: the king appoints 10 members, the House of Representatives elects 35, and an electoral college elects 15, three from each developmental region. Bills may be introduced in either house except finance bills, which are introduced only by the lower house. All bills must be passed by both houses and then receive royal assent. If the upper house rejects a bill, the lower house may override. If the king returns a bill for reconsideration, a joint session of parliament may pass the bill, which then automatically receives royal assent within 30 days. The king may promulgate ordinances, but only when both houses of parliament are not in session, and such ordinances are not effective until approved by both houses. The king may dissolve the House of Representatives for a period of six months, after which new elections must be held, but the National Assembly is a permanent body. Nevertheless, King Gyanendra dissolved both houses in May 2002.

Judicial Branch: The 1990 constitution is the fundamental law of the land and establishes a three-tier court system consisting of 75 district courts, 16 appellate courts, and the Supreme Court. Village and municipal bodies may exercise quasi-judicial functions for minor offenses. All courts have original jurisdiction, but district courts have original jurisdiction over most judicial matters. The Supreme Court also has appellate jurisdiction and jurisdiction over all courts, except military courts, and Supreme Court orders, decisions, and interpretations are binding on all, including the king. The Supreme Court has a chief justice appointed by the king on the recommendation of the Constitutional Council and 14 judges appointed by the king on the recommendation of the Judicial Council, which also appoints appellate and district court judges. The House of Representatives can impeach Supreme Court justices. The judiciary is widely regarded as becoming more autonomous, but it suffers from large case backlogs, insufficient finances and personnel, political intervention, poor demarcation of jurisdiction between courts, and biases based on caste and economic status. Thus, many Nepalese do not view the official court system as a viable option for legal matters. A survey conducted in 2000 revealed that the majority of legal-type issues were handled not by government officials but by local actors, such as village chiefs.

Judicial and Legal System: Nepal's legal system is composed of the 1990 constitution, the legal code, legislation, and Supreme Court precedents. The constitution guarantees equality of all citizens and provides fundamental rights and liberties. The legal code, or Muluki Ain, was introduced in 1854 and revised in 1963. It combines Hindu laws and sanctions, British and Indian codes, and traditional rules of behavior among the Newars in the Kathmandu Valley. Issues not covered by this code, however, are dealt with according to customs of local communities. Nepal does not have separate criminal and civil courts. Judges decide all cases and have wide discretion in doing so. The constitution does not provide for trial by jury but does provide rights to counsel and public trial as well as protection from double indemnity and retroactive application of laws.

Administrative Divisions: Nepal's largest administrative divisions are development regions, which are divided into zones. Zones are further divided into districts, which in turn are divided into nine to 17 *ilakas* that cover clusters of villages and municipalities. Municipalities and villages are divided into wards, the smallest administrative unit, with villages containing nine wards and municipalities nine to 35 wards depending on population. Nepal has a total of five development regions, 14 zones, 75 districts, 58 municipalities, 3,915 villages, and 36,032 wards. Municipalities and villages are legally distinguished by population. Municipalities must have a minimum population of 20,000, except in mountain and hill areas, where the minimum population is 10,000.

Provincial and Local Government: Government below the national level is complex, evolving, and a highly debated political topic. All administrative divisions have one or more governing bodies, and members are directly elected, indirectly elected, or appointed by the central government. The king appoints regional and zonal administrators, who are responsible for coordinating the functions of ministries and departments within their respective areas. Villages, municipalities, and districts each have two governing bodies that are composed of directly and indirectly elected members serving five-year terms, with some representatives serving simultaneously on two or more governing bodies. One governing body at each level meets once per month and is responsible for implementing central government policies but also has autonomous policy, revenues, and judicial authority. The other governing body at the same level meets once or twice per year to approve the corresponding body's policies, budgets, and revenue methods. Wards have one governing body, a ward committee whose members also serve on municipal and village committees and councils.

The central government has expressed interest in enhancing the provision of public services by enabling local bodies to have fiscal and policy-making capabilities to provide such services. However, many ministries have been criticized for not delegating relevant functions to local bodies, and critics contend that central government appointees that serve on district, village, and municipality bodies have compromised the autonomy of those bodies. Furthermore, local bodies are believed to be particularly weak in their mobilization and management of financial resources, with many depending on the central government for long-term investment. In addition, the functioning of local governments has been severely undermined by the lack of officials to serve on those bodies. King Gyanendra suspended district, village, and municipal elections in 2002, and many officials subsequently appointed to those bodies have resigned. In July 2005, Nepal's Election Commission announced that municipal elections would be held in April 2006, but political parties had previously announced that they would boycott elections called by the king.

Electoral System: Nepal has universal suffrage for citizens 18 years of age and older. The minimum age to run for office is 21 for local offices, 25 for the House of Representatives, and 35 for the National Assembly. Members of village development committees and municipalities are directly elected and constitute an electoral college that elects district development committee members. A district's number of representatives for national office is proportional to the district's population, and the number of representatives for district and local offices is based on area, population, and other factors.

The Electoral Commission oversees elections and political parties. Elections were held in 1991, 1994, and 1999, but elections scheduled for November 13, 2002, remain suspended. From 1991 to 1999, the number of voters increased from 11.2 million to 13.5 million, and turnout remained at nearly 65 percent. Although the number of voters in 1999 was evenly split between males and females, only 143 of the 2,238 candidates for the House of Representatives were women, and just 12 women were elected. In the same election, there were 205 election constituencies, 6,821 polling centers, and 100 political parties, 39 of which stood for election. Parties' election expenditures are legally limited. To run for office, a party must have received 3 percent of votes in the previous parliamentary election, and 5 percent of its candidates must be women.

Politics and Political Parties: Since the restoration of democracy in 1990, political parties have been among the most influential actors in politics, but their popularity and effectiveness are generally seen as declining. In February 2005, the king suspended all parties, claiming they were not effectively addressing the civil conflict, yet the suspension's constitutionality is debated. For many reasons, political parties have seldom been capable of challenging the king's power and have rarely mobilized large portions of the population. The parties are frequently perceived as representing distinct social identities, often those of dominant caste/ethnic groups. Competition within and among parties is common and is often perceived as based on personal interests rather than on ideology or policy. Many actions of parties and their members appear to be oriented to acquiring and maintaining power. As measured by votes received in the 1999 election, the most popular parties were the Nepali Congress (36.1 percent), Nepali Communist Party (30.7 percent), and Rastriya Prajatantra Party (10.1 percent).

Mass Media: Historically, radio has been the most prevalent means of mass communication. Government-owned Radio Nepal has been the sole domestic radio provider since 1951, and by

1995 it was broadcasting in short-wave, medium-wave, and FM frequencies. Private operators can lease the FM channel, and there are plans to establish FM stations outside the capital. Television programming commenced in 1985, and broadcasters include government-owned Nepal Television, which has two channels, and private broadcasters Nepal One, Shangri-La, and Space Time Network. All private television broadcasters have experienced financial losses and content restrictions. Foreign programs can be accessed via satellite or cable. Statistics on viewership are not available, but it is estimated at less than 15 percent of the population. According to government figures, in 2003 Nepal had 3,741 registered newspapers, of which 251 were published daily. Government-owned *Gorkhapatra* (Gorkha Journal) had the highest daily circulation at around 75,000. Most registered newspapers were published either weekly (1,304) or monthly (1,122). Most vernacular news media are regarded as having little credibility as a result of affiliations with political parties.

Foreign Relations: Constitutionally, foreign policy is to be guided by "the principles of the United Nations Charter, nonalignment, Panchsheel [five principles of peaceful coexistence], international law and the value of world peace." In practice, foreign policy has not been directed toward projecting influence internationally but toward preserving autonomy and addressing domestic economic and security issues. Nepal's most substantive international relations are perhaps with international economic institutions, such as the Asian Development Bank, the International Monetary Fund, the World Bank, and the South Asian Association for Regional Cooperation, a multilateral economic development association. Nepal also has strong bilateral relations with major providers of economic and military aid, such as France, Germany, Japan, Switzerland, the United States, and particularly the United Kingdom, with whom military ties date to the nineteenth century. The country also maintains strong political relations with India and China, usually attempting to balance one against the other. However, relations with India are fraught with trade and border disputes and Indian suspicions that Nepalese and Pakistani rebels use Nepal as a haven to attack India. Relations with Bhutan have been strained since 1992 over the nationality and possible repatriation of refugees from Bhutan.

Membership in International Organizations: Nepal is a member of numerous international organizations including: the Asian Development Bank; Bangladesh, India, Myanmar, Sri Lanka, Thailand Economic Cooperation; Colombo Plan; Food and Agriculture Organization of the United Nations; Group of 77; International Bank for Reconstruction and Development; International Centre for Settlement of Investment Disputes; International Chamber of Commerce; International Civil Aviation Organization; International Criminal Police Organization; International Development Association; International Federation of Red Cross and Red Crescent Societies; International Finance Corporation; International Fund for Agricultural Development; International Labour Organization; International Maritime Organization; International Monetary Fund; International Olympic Committee; International Organization for Migration (observer); International Organization for Standardization; International Telecommunication Union; Mulitlateral Investment Guarantee Association; Nonaligned Movement; Organisation for the Prohibition of Chemical Weapons; South Asia Cooperative Environment Program; South Asian Association for Regional Cooperation; United Nations (UN); UN Educational, Scientific and Cultural Organization; UN Industrial Development Organization; Universal Postal Union; World Bank; World Customs Organization; World Health

Organization; World Intellectual Property Organization; World Meteorological Organization, World Tourism Organization, and World Trade Organization.

Major International Treaties: Nepal is a signatory to numerous international treaties including: the Basel Convention on the Control of Transboundary Movements of Hazardous Wastes and Their Disposal; Chemical Weapons Convention; Comprehensive Nuclear Test Ban Treaty (signed but not ratified as of September 2005); Convention against Torture and Other Cruel, Inhuman or Degrading Treatment or Punishment; Convention on Biological Diversity; Convention on Fishing and Conservation of Living Resources of the High Seas (signed but not ratified as of September 2005); Convention on International Trade in Endangered Species of Wild Flora and Fauna; Convention on the Elimination of All Forms of Discrimination Against Women; Convention on the Elimination of All Forms of Racial Discrimination; Convention on the Rights of the Child; Convention on Wetlands of International Importance Especially as Waterfowl Habitat; Covenant on Economic, Social and Cultural Rights; Geneva Protocol; International Atomic Energy Association Safeguards Agreement; International Covenant of Civil and Political Rights; International Tropical Timber Agreement 1983; International Tropical Timber Agreement 1994; Montreal Protocol on Substances that Deplete the Ozone layer; Treaty Banning Nuclear Weapon Tests in the Atmosphere, in Outer Space, and Under Water; Treaty on the Non-Proliferation of Nuclear Weapons; United Nations Convention to Combat Desertification; United Nations Convention on the Law of the Sea; and United Nations Framework Convention on Climate Change.

NATIONAL SECURITY

Armed Forces Overview: Nepal has only one military service, the Royal Nepalese Army (RNA). The army's stated purpose is to protect Nepal from external threats, but because its capabilities are far smaller than those of neighboring China and India, the government historically has used diplomacy rather than force to maintain territorial integrity. The RNA has been mostly involved in ceremonial functions, international peacekeeping, and supporting the monarchy against domestic opposition. The army also is engaged in domestic noncombat activities, such as infrastructure development, nature conservation, and disaster relief. Since 2002, however, the army has been active in a civil war against Maoist rebels who have severely tested its reputation and capabilities. The RNA's limited resources have constrained its ability to protect infrastructure from the Maoists, and the RNA has had to use commercially leased helicopters to improve its limited mobility. The government is attempting to improve the RNA's capabilities, and the defense budget has increased substantially since 2000.

According to the 1990 constitution, the king is the supreme commander of the army and appoints the commander in chief (the chief of army staff, or COAS) on the prime minister's recommendation. The king may control the army on the recommendation of the National Defense Council, which consists of the COAS, the minister of defense, and the prime minister, who serves as chairman. However, the king's suspension of the government in February 2005 terminated the prime minister's military powers, at least temporarily. The COAS delegates operational functions to various generals and principal staff officers but personally directs the army's Research and Development Directorate, Defense Ordnance Productions Directorate, and

Development Construction Directorate. The Military Intelligence Directorate and the National Defense Council are primarily responsible for intelligence activities. Directly responsible to the COAS are the chief of general staff (CGS) and the chief of staff (COS). The CGS is the head of "G" Branch and is primarily responsible for operations, intelligence, and training, each of which is organized in individual directorates. The COS is responsible for military operations other than war, which include United Nations peacekeeping operations, nature conservation and wildlife preservation, and the army's welfare organizations. The COS has approximately 4,400 army troops under his direct control.

Foreign Military Relations: Nepalese serve in both the British and Indian armies, but Nepal has no formal military links with other countries or intergovernmental organizations other than the United Nations. Since 2001, India, the United Kingdom, the United States, and other governments have provided various forms of assistance to combat the Maoist rebels.

External Threat: Nepal faces no threats from another country's regular military forces.

Defense Budget: Nepal's defense budget and expenditures have grown substantially, although exact figures vary by source. According to the Ministry of Finance, from fiscal year (FY) 2001 to FY2005 Ministry of Defense expenditures grew from US$51.5 million to an estimated US$109.9 million. The Ministry of Defense has been budgeted approximately US$149.8 million for FY2006, but its expenditures often exceed its budget. In FY2004, for example, the defense budget was US$97.3 million but defense expenditures were US$110.5 million.

Major Military Units: Nepal has an army but no navy, coast guard, marines, or air force. Command and control of the military has undergone significant changes since 1990, and in 2001 the Royal Nepalese Army (RNA) shifted from a brigade-based structure to one based on divisions. There are six combat divisions, each responsible for a particular area (Far-Western, Mid-Western, Western, Central, Eastern, and Valley), and each includes combat brigades, combat support, and combat service support units. One combat brigade is designated as the Royal Guards Brigade, and there are separate aviation, paratrooper, and special operations brigades. Each brigade contains two to three infantry battalions (logistics, rifles, and support) and several independent infantry companies, such as air defense, artillery, engineers, field ambulance, light artillery, ordnance, repair, and signals. Foreign observers estimate that in 2003 the army had between 63,000 and 85,000 active-duty personnel, including nearly 320 personnel in the Royal Nepal Army Air Wing (RNAAW). The army has no reserve component.

Major Military Equipment: In 2004 the army was believed to have 40 reconnaissance vehicles, 40 armored personnel carriers, six 75-millimeter artillery missiles, five 94-millimeter mountain artillery missiles, 14 105-millimeter artillery missiles, 70 120-millimeter mortars, a publicly unavailable number of 107-millimeter M30 mortars, 30 PRC Type 56 14.5-millimeter light antiaircraft guns, an unknown number of 37-millimeter light antiaircraft guns, and two 40-millimeter antiaircraft guns. The air wing had one BAe–748 aircraft and one Skyvan as well as 11 helicopters but no combat aircraft or armed helicopters.

Military Service: The minimum age for military service is 18. Women are eligible for military service, but most serve in noncombat positions.

Paramilitary Forces: The Armed Police Force (APF) was established in January 2001 as a subordinate unit of the Ministry of Home Affairs, which reportedly created some tensions between the ministry and the army. The APF has a force of approximately 15,000 personnel, and its primary function is internal security, particularly to contain the Maoist insurgency. Other duties include VIP security and assisting the Nepal Police in maintenance of law and order.

Foreign Military Forces: The British Gurkhas Nepal, a British Army organization, has 63 personnel engaged in recruitment, pension payment, and other administrative services for Nepalese that serve or have served in the British Army as part of the Brigade of Gurkhas.

Military Forces Abroad: The prestigious reputation of Nepalese soldiers is due in no small part to their foreign service. The Indian army has 40,000 Nepalese, and approximately 3,300 Nepalese serve in the British Army's Brigade of Gurkhas. The number of Nepalese in the British Army has declined from the 8,000 that served in 1998 but remains one of Nepal's most important sources of foreign exchange. Nepalese in the Brigade of Gurkhas may serve anywhere that British soldiers do, except Northern Ireland. Currently, all units of the Brigade of Gurkhas are stationed in the United Kingdom except the Gurkha battalion in Brunei, the British Gurkhas Nepal, and—through an arrangement with the British Army—the Gurkha Contingent of the Singapore Police Force.

Nepal is a member of the United Nations (UN) Disengagement Observer Force, and Nepalese troops also have been active in multilateral forces under UN auspices. As of January 2005, Nepal was the world's fourth largest contributor of troops to peacekeeping missions, with 3,016 troops serving in various international peacekeeping operations. Since 1958, nearly 46,000 Nepalese troops have participated in 29 missions. As of 2005, Nepalese troops were serving in Burundi, Côte d'Ivoire, Democratic Republic of the Congo, Eritrea and Ethiopia, Haiti, Israel and Syria, Kosovo, Liberia, the Middle East, and Sudan. Nepalese troops also have served in numerous other UN peacekeeping operations.

Police: The Nepal Police are under the direction of the Ministry of Home Affairs. According to the Nepal Police, in 2004 there were 47,349 police personnel, including 27,912 constables. The Ministry of Home Affairs also administers the 15,000-strong Armed Police Force, which is involved primarily in domestic counterinsurgency other than law enforcement. In fiscal year 2005, the government allocated US$101.7 million to the police.

Internal Security and Terrorism: There are allegations that Nepalese territory is used as a haven by Islamic militants either from or supported by Pakistan and al Qaeda. Yet, it is unclear whether those militants pose a threat to Nepalese security or are primarily a threat to India. Unquestionably, the civil conflict is the gravest threat to Nepal's internal security and possibly its existence. Estimates of the conflict's economic impact vary, but the Ministry of Finance claims tourism, banking, social services, and physical infrastructure have suffered considerably. The rebels are members of the Communist Party of Nepal (Maoist)—CPN(M)—and are led by Puspakamal Dahal, alias Prachanda, and Babu Ram Bhattarai. Their stated goals include establishment of a constituent assembly to draft a new constitution, land reform, establishment of Nepal as a secular nation, termination of several treaties with India, and abolition of untouchability. The Nepalese and many foreign governments categorize the CPN(M) as a terrorist organization that seeks to establish a communist dictatorship. It has an estimated 5,000 regular armed members and approximately 10,000 to 15,000 members in local militias. Observers contend that most members and supporters are indigenous groups, *dalits* ("broken people" or untouchables), and lower castes. There is evidence of CPN(M) collusion with Maoists and other rebels in India as well as allegations of arms purchases from the Liberation Tigers of Tamil Eelam (LTTE) in Sri Lanka.

The current conflict began on February 13, 1996, and by 2005 the CPN(M) had control over an estimated 40 to 60 percent of the country. Most fighting has occurred in rural areas and in western districts. Until early 2000, Nepalese police efforts against the CPN(M) were generally uncoordinated. The army became involved in February 2000 and began actively engaging the CPN(M) in November 2001. Security forces generally have been hobbled by their lack of funds, local support, and counterinsurgency experience, while the mountainous, forested, generally roadless terrain favors the Maoists' guerrilla tactics. Human rights observers and foreign governments have suggested that some government efforts to address the conflict—including the suspension of civil liberties and elected government—have reduced the government's popular legitimacy and thus have been counterproductive. The Maoists' attacks on infrastructure reportedly have lowered their popular support, as have accusations of robbery, extortion, and forced recruiting. The CPN(M), however, claims such activities are either unauthorized actions committed by lower-level cadres or are justified to prevent the use of public resources to exploit Nepalese. Peace talks in 2001 and 2003 were unsuccessful.

Independent observers contend that a significant portion of the rural population is supportive of the insurgents' goals but has grown exasperated with repressive activities of both the Maoists and the government. Indeed, unarmed civilians have been frequent victims. According to a Nepalese human rights organization, the Informal Service Sector Centre, from February 13, 1996, to September 16, 2005, 12,809 persons were killed in the conflict, with 64 percent attributed to security forces, 36 percent to the CPN(M), and 82 percent of all conflict-related deaths occurring since 2002. Of the killings attributed to security forces, most were of actual or suspected members of the CPN(M) or political parties (65 percent) or agricultural workers (15.6 percent). Of the killings attributed to the Maoists, most were of police personnel (28.2 percent), agricultural workers (16.2 percent), army personnel (14.4 percent), or civil servants (11.6 percent). Additionally, 50,356 persons had been displaced by the conflict through 2004. However, these figures include only verified events; actual numbers may be higher.

Human Rights: Historically, civil liberties have been limited, but Nepal's government has not been regarded as among the world's worst violators of human rights. Nevertheless, human rights violations have increased substantially since the escalation of civil conflict in 2000, and security forces engaged in substantial numbers of these human rights violations prior to the civil conflict. According to the United Nations (UN), Nepal leads the world in arbitrary abduction and detention by security forces in large part as a result of the civil conflict. The conflict between the Communist Party of Nepal (Maoist) and government security forces has resulted in numerous allegations of human rights violations by both sides, with most victims being unarmed civilian noncombatants. The Maoists have been accused of unlawful killings, torture, and nearly 36,849 abductions. Security forces have been accused of disappearances, unlawful killings, arbitrary arrests, torture, and obstructing both courts and human rights investigations—all with impunity.

However, about one-third of those abducted by security forces were released after months in secret detention, and in July 2004 the government created a committee to locate the disappeared.

Outside of the conflict, civil liberties are tenuous, and human rights abuses are common. Discrimination on the basis of caste, gender, ethnicity, and sexuality is ubiquitous, and domestic violence, forced labor, and forced prostitution are pervasive. However, various organizations have emerged to address the needs of persons suffering discrimination. Still, civil liberties such as freedom of speech, press, and lawful assembly have been severely curtailed with King Gyanendra's suspension of the constitution in February 2005. The government also has been criticized for ratifying human rights treaties and conventions but not incorporating human rights laws into legislation. Indeed, there are no laws against domestic violence or police torture, and the police are accused of excessive force and corruption. Because of poor communication, police outside the capital often have tremendous autonomy and discretion in handling law and order matters and often do so in ways not consistent with the law.